UNCLE TOM'S
BABBLIN'

Uncle Tom's Babblin'

Tom McCollough

UNCLE TOM'S BABBLIN'

iUniverse books may be ordered through booksellers or by contacting:

iUniverse LLC
1663 Liberty Drive
Bloomington, IN 47403
www.iuniverse.com
1-800-Authors (1-800-288-4677)

ISBN: 978-1-4917-4577-9 (sc)
ISBN: 978-1-4917-4578-6 (e)

Library of Congress Control Number: 2014915624

Printed in the United States of America.

iUniverse rev. date: 09/04/2014

To everyone else:

old friends

new friends

helpful employees

other helpers

doctors

lawyers

Indian chiefs

And for the second time, Marian, Elizabeth, Janice, Alex, Donn, and Sharon.

And to my faithful commentator, Bob Ballus.

CONTENTS

Preface 1

What's Good about Being Eighty-Five 3

You Are Getting Sleepy 4

Living on the Edge..6

Talking Points...9

The Day the Ceiling Fell.. 11

Bird-Watching.. 13

On Reading a Good Book.. 16

The Cliché Expert... 18

The Good Vampire 21

Antiques..25

Games We Play 30

Government as Theater (2013) 33

Poignant Moments Recently.......................................36

Nuts to You..37

Residing n the Arms of Morpheus.............................39

Sana Mente, Sanum Corpore 41

Where Is the Damn Car? 43

The Eyes Have It..45

The Sweater from the Isle of Iona 47

Peekaboo, I See You 50

The Cloak-and-Dagger Game 52

My Older Siblings: the Twins, Jack and Jim 55

Honey, I'm Home..58

I Ain't Sick, Yet 60

A Cat's Affection 64

I Love Coffee, I Love Tea … 65

War and Pieces..68

Steak 71

Thou Shall Not Eat French Fries.............................73

Suggestions from Friends..77

The Torture of a Thousand Drops of Water 80

There's a Hole in My Bucket 82

Let's Stay in Touch...86

Things Fall Apart..89

Money, Money, Money 91

Afterword..95

PREFACE

My nephew, Hal Samuelson, showed his two little girls a copy of my last book, *I Lied, There's More,* by explaining that this was Uncle Tom's babbling. Exactly. I decided immediately to make that the next title of any forthcoming book.

During the last few months, I have reread all four of my previous books. The writing is uneven—sometimes well done, sometimes boring, often repetitious. As a memoir, the books reveal a hefty amount of what has happened in my long life. Most of my stories have been told. Nothing in them is earth-shattering, nor do they require hours of concentration. Many people have noted that they enjoyed being able to pick up the books, read briefly, and fall asleep.

Now freed of most of my life stories, I can write mindlessly on current fads, news, politics, and popular culture. (Now I can get it off my chest.) These days I feel that society is floundering and that yesteryear was better than now. My ennui probably comes from being eighty-five years old, with little interest in rekindling a need to improve or manage things. They legalized liquor, voted dry, and then repealed Prohibition. All things change. Life is a moving target.

Dear reader, thank you for putting up with all this nonsense.

Tom McCollough
Summer 2014

What's Good about Being Eighty-Five

I don't care who wins the Oscars.
I can stay up as long as I like.
I don't have to dress before eleven in the morning.
I can be grumpy, and no one cares.
I've been there before.
I've outlived most of those mean SOBs.
I still have most of my teeth.
I don't have to wear a tie.
I don't have to have any more colonoscopies.
I can ignore politicians and hang up on unsolicited calls.
I have a *few* great friends.
I beat the odds.

AMEN

You Are Getting Sleepy

During the 1930s, it was not unusual that a vaudeville show would include a hypnotist. He would ask for volunteers from the audience and seat ten or fifteen of them on chairs on the stage. He began his spiel by saying "You are getting sleepy" in a persistent voice. Not every subject succumbed, but many did. Soon, about half the volunteers were slouched over sound asleep, and the show proceeded. He would have them purr like cats, conduct imaginary orchestras, imagine they were hungry, etc.

As a little boy, the performance seemed miraculous and very scary. I was fascinated and curious. Could I do that?

When I was a college freshman, I bought a short, ten-cent pamphlet entitled *How to Hypnotize*. Everything in the text followed what I remembered from past vaudeville days.

On a Saturday morning, I went to the biology lab to complete a frog dissection. A fellow student was sitting across from me. I told him that I had recently studied hypnotism. Would he like to try it?

"Why not?" he answered.

In my most persuasive voice, I said, "You are getting sleepy," as I dangled my keys in front of his face. Within minutes, he was slumped and sound asleep. Oh my God, what had I done? What if he wouldn't wake up? Would I be kicked out of college? Where could I go for help? Terror!

I had no choice but to proceed. "You are a dog. Bark!" The fellow barked. "You are sad and will cry." Tears poured down his face. *Oh my God, it's working,* I thought.

Now for the big finale. "After I count to ten, you will wake up and remember nothing. But ten seconds after you awake, you will feel hot." I held my breath, hoping that he would wake up with no consequences. "Ten, nine, eight, seven, six, five, four, three, two, one!"

The fellow stirred and stared at me. Ten seconds later, he started to sweat. Even my posthypnotic suggestion had worked. I was never as afraid as I was at that moment. I didn't know what to say, so we both continued dissecting our frogs.

Every time I saw the fellow again, either in class or around campus, I had this weird feeling that I had done something wrong and that I would be punished. I never attempted to do it again, and no one ever knew.

"You are getting sleepy"—not because I am hypnotizing you, but because it is time for your afternoon nap.

Living on the Edge

A study in 2006 concluded that the San Andreas Fault has reached a sufficient stress level for the next "big one," greater than 7.0 on the Richter Scale to occur. It also concluded that the risk of a large earthquake may be increasing more rapidly than researchers had previously thought.

Wikipedia

Oh my, I am living on the edge of the San Andreas Fault near Saratoga, California. The tectonic plate could slip any day now, and all of the paintings in our apartment could crash to the floor. We could be without electricity and water for days. We hope that our building will not fall down, but that will depend on the severity of the quake. This is no laughing matter.

Being of a cautious nature, I am prepared. I have a windup radio and a windup flashlight in the nightstand. We have water stored under the bed and a closet full of food in pull-tab cans. Flashlights are stashed in every room, and I have a whistle to signal the rescuers.

But I worry whether any rescuers would arrive in a timely manner. We live in a retirement community with hundreds of residents. The earthquake will probably occur in the middle of the night, when most staff are at home and unable to use the highways because the overpasses have fallen. I also assume that the residents in the healthcare center would be the first to be helped; those in assisted living would be aided next because some of us need oxygen, insulin, and electric scooters to get around. Pity the poor folks who live independently; they can get along by themselves without help—unless they have been knocked helpless by a falling bookcase or an errant couch.

I am a seasoned earthquake participant. Years ago I was at a seminar at Asilomar Conference Center in Pacific Grove, California. Suddenly the overstuffed chair I was sitting in started to shimmy, and we all hollered, "Earthquake!" No damage done, just a nice, mellow, little one.

I was once a consultant for a USAID educational experiment in San Salvador. My office on the second floor of an office building had a desk that would wiggle a bit every day. I assumed it was from the heavy traffic on the traffic circle below. The tremors continued day after day and at all hours. The project leader told me that they experienced at least nineteen small earthquakes every day. Puny little things.

The biggest quake I ever felt was in Las Vegas. We were housed on the seventeenth floor of the Showboat Hotel packing for the trip home when the room started to shake violently. I was in the bathroom shaving, and Marian was by the bed. I called to her, and she had to crawl to meet me in a doorway. We heard people shouting in the hallway. I became worried that we might have to carry our luggage down seventeen floors if the elevator failed. After several minutes, the swaying stopped and the chandelier came to rest. The elevator worked, and we left for the airport. An aftershock disrupted departure, but we eventually made it back to Ohio.

While I fear how we might fare if the "big one" happens while we are living in Saratoga, it would amuse me to see California float off into the Pacific Ocean. Maps dating from 1539 show California as an island.

It could happen again.

Talking Points

Many years ago, I was sent to have a conversation with the medical advisor to President Jimmy Carter in the White House. The fellow's office was in a small, crowded, windowless office in the White House basement.

Before going, I was advised by our Abbott lobbyist that it was essential that I have a one-page document called "talking points" for the interview. After saying hello, the protocol was to hand the person your talking points. After he read them, a conversation could proceed. All this was necessary to save time, focus the topic, and prevent surprises for the executive. In many subsequent congressional interviews, I was prepared with my one-page talking points to kick off the exchange.

Writing the talking points document was a challenge. One talking point? Not enough. Ten talking points? Too many. Put the most important point first or last? Size of type? My first experience with talking points was a revelation.

Trying to focus your thoughts has appeal. Life is complex with many shades of gray, but the arc of life is not. Born, live, die. What if you were required to write your biography as talking points? What would you write? Here are my biographic talking points:

- born and raised by a loving mother and father

- married a supportive, guileless wife
- raised two bright, energetic children
- had an interesting career
- worked for a demanding boss who made sure I had ample stock options
- had some serious health problems
- retired in beautiful California
- lived happily as I waited for the inevitable, final talking point

The yin-yang of life often produces half ups and half downs. I believe my life has had more ups than downs. (Perhaps I don't understand a working definition of *ups* and *downs*.)

Individual events don't count for much. They add color to your life but are unimportant in the long run. I remember being frightened getting into a dilapidated taxi in New Delhi and whisked off to a rundown hotel a half hour away. Does that count as a down or warrant a talking point? No, but it was memorable.

As for talking points, try writing your biography in ten talking points or less. It might surprise you.

The Day the Ceiling Fell

In 1961 we bought a ninety-three-acre hill farm in Perry County, Ohio, for a weekend retreat. The house was a hundred years old but had good bones. The frame was solid oak with poplar siding. The first floor had been modified slightly, having had one wall removed from one of the two front parlors to form a larger living room. The house was completely livable when we moved in.

We had no need to make many changes, but we slowly began to improve some of the cosmetic things that needed attention. Many of the walls had faded wallpaper that was soiled and torn in places. I covered the dining room walls with burlap to add more sturdiness to the old plaster and painted the burlap white above the dado. The living room's eleven-foot ceiling also had wallpaper on it and some cracks showing in the plaster. That year, 1961, was during the era of textured paint, and I decided to paint the ceiling with sand paint to give it strength and a more tasteful appearance.

The weekend I painted the ceiling, we were visited by Marian's mother and father. Frankly, Marian's mother questioned my suitability as a husband for her first born. I was a bit too wacky and not sufficiently attentive to her aggressive advice about *everything*. I was not her favorite.

That Saturday morning, I mixed the fine sand into the white paint and started painting in the corner. I finished about noon, and we sat down to lunch.

Suddenly I heard a strange ripping noise, and I ran to the living room where the sound was coming from. I was horrified to find the ceiling wallpaper sagging in the middle and slowly edging toward the side walls. It was slow-motion chaos. I ran for a case cutter, climbed a ladder, and started cutting the heavy, wet, ceiling wallpaper where it met the side walls. I had just finished cutting when the whole ceiling paint job fell to the floor. The family and in-laws watched the disaster. My beloved mother-in-law had a sinister smirk on her face. I had just proven her correct. I was an idiot.

It took all afternoon to clean up the mess. The exposed plaster ceiling revealed some severe cracks and other imperfections. I had uncovered even more serious problems. The next week, I spackled and sanded the cracks, and the following weekend I painted the ceiling white—very carefully.

My mother-in-law and I never did form a lovey-dovey relationship, but why did fate let her be present in one of my darkest moments?

Kismet can be cruel.

BIRD-WATCHING

Do you have a favorite bird? Are you cuckoo about cuckoos? Do you own a derelict, hardback copy of Roger Tory Peterson's *Birds of North America* that is losing its cover? If so, you may qualify as an avid bird watcher.

Do you remember as a child the thrill of the sight of the first robin in the spring digging for a worm and tugging it up? Do you become breathless watching the eastern towhee scooting leaves ahead as he searches for bugs? Does the sight of the bluebird swooping down to catch an insect in midflight thrill you? Do you maintain three bird feeders with differing seeds or sugar water to attract different types of birds? If any of these behaviors pertain, you are a bird aficionado. Join the club.

My wife, children, and I were not serious birders until we moved to the country. We observed many birds we had never seen before: cedar waxwings, kingfishers, vireos, red-shouldered hawks, and others. Our property was mostly wooded, and we learned that different species either lived in the woods or in the open fields.

Bird watchers attract other bird watchers. When the migrating warblers came through in May, we invited friends for an annual bird walk. The experts were able to identify warblers by their song instead of sight. (For city dwellers, warblers are about the size of a sparrow and usually come in shades of green and yellow. About twenty varieties look alike and require an eagle eye to distinguish one from another.) They migrate through Ohio in the spring and fall.

Most birds are limited to geographic areas. When we went to Sanibel in Florida, we learned that wintering song birds were found in the Bailey Tract, but the marsh birds were in the Ding Darling National Wildlife Refuge: the rare white pelicans, the roseate spoonbills, anhingas, herons, egrets, and a mess of ducks. We had an osprey nest in front of our condo and watched the adult birds circle overhead at daybreak until they dove into the bay to pluck a fish from the surface. Occasionally we spotted the three-foot-tall wood stork, one of the ugliest birds on earth. When the wood stork sits, it plops down on its butt with its feet stretched out in front. They look ridiculous, but their black and white flight plumage is magnificent.

Normal bird watchers carry binoculars, typically 7x power. That magnification offers a spacious field of vision and easy observation. Avid birdwatchers buy 10x binoculars that require quick observation. Really nutty birdwatchers buy even higher magnification but require a tripod to steady the device. Warblers flit nervously and never become still. Any magnification over 7x is a liability.

Many birdwatchers maintain a life list of all species they have seen. In time the list grows extensive, but the unseen birds are more exotic. Expensive travel budgets are required to go where the chances are higher of spotting a rarity. A safari to Costa Rica may be necessary. Marian and I never reached that level of interest.

At the Saratoga retirement community, we watch squawking crows, some pigeons, and an occasional humming bird. Other birds are heard nearby.

Neither Marian nor I tweet!

On Reading a Good Book

About half the books I read are hardbacks, and the other half are on my electronic Kindle. In fact I own six Kindles. My wife has one of them, and my daughter has one I bought. I use the newer Kindle Fire, and I have no idea where the older white one has gone. When I buy an e-book, I download the book to all of the Kindles so that three people can read them for the price of one. Purist readers like to smell printer's ink, but I can enlarge the size of the type on the Kindle so I don't have to squint.

The most widely read books at our retirement community library are mysteries. What is the appeal of a whodunit? Intrigue, cleverness, escapism, suspense, and they're often well written. The genre has wide scope, ranging from shoot-'em-ups to elaborate historical page turners such as *The Da Vinci Code* by Dan Brown. Most serious readers have a favorite mystery author who turns out a book a year, and the writer becomes rich and famous, like John Grisham, John le Carre, Mary Higgins Clark, and Tom Clancy.

A glut of books are published every year—literally hundreds of thousands. You couldn't begin to read everything published.

With so many options, what should you select to read: new books, old books, fiction, nonfiction, biography, classics, history, mysteries? It's a matter of personal preference. My personal preference is for nonfiction. However, if a novel gets rave reviews and remains on best-seller lists for months, it means that it might be worth considering.

One of my responsibilities when I was chairman of our library committee was to buy new books. I read two or three best-seller lists every week, read reviews, and responded to resident requests.

On average I read about two books a month, but I no longer attend a book club. I was the only male among fifteen readers, and their choice of books often did not interest me.

What I love about the reading experience is the magic moment that happens when you become transported, mesmerized, involved, and you literally do not want to put the book down or the book to end. You don't want to stop to eat, you don't want to go to a doctor's appointment or to a committee meeting. The world closes in, and you just want to read undisturbed. I hope you have often enjoyed that feeling.

It's magic.

THE CLICHÉ EXPERT

On August 31, 1951, a staff humorist at the *New Yorker*, Frank Sullivan, wrote his first article about the "cliché expert." He invented a droll human, Mr. Skip Arbuthnot, who would "write" essays over the next twenty years. "In one essay Mr. Arbuthnot was asked what he did for exercise. He replied, 'I keep the wolf from the door, let the cat out of the bag, take the bull by the horns, count my chickens before they are hatched, and see that the horse isn't put behind the cart or stolen before I lock the barn door.'"

Over many years, Mr. Arbuthnot commented on political campaigns, atomic energy, baseball, and other topics using only clichés to explain his point of view. I discovered Frank Sullivan in the sixties and was delighted by his wit and intelligence. Thereafter, I started to search for clichés in common usage. For example:

avoid it like the plague
dead as a doornail
take the tiger by the tail
if only the walls could talk
think outside the box
like a kid in a candy store

There are hundreds of others that inhabit our speech and writing patterns. I am overly cliché sensitive.

Language is always in flux. Old clichés fade from current usage, and others become fashionable. Currently, some are used so frequently they become tiresome and irritating. Like these:

"I've Got Your Back"

This cliché has become so ubiquitous that insurance advertisers are using it in ads to make a company sound contemporary. To me it sounds as if the copywriter is fourteen years old. Its meaning? "I will protect you." Why not say that?

"Back in the Day"

My favorite cable reality show is *Pawn Stars,* during which people bring in unusual items to the store to pawn or sell. Many of the items are antiques: toys, guns, jewelry, art, or other treasure from the attic. The middle-aged proprietor or the grandpa, attempting to explain the item to the audience, will say, "Back in the day …" But I am also hearing the phrase in other TV shows. Why not say, "In the sixteenth century" or "In 1910"?

"He's Trying to Get His Mojo Back"

What the hell is a *mojo*? It means charm, talent, and the ability to get things done, and folks are always trying to find it or get it back. Teenagers and the streetwise use the phrase in conversation. *Mojo* is a useful word, but I had to look up its origin and felt inferior for doing so.

Do I ever "fall from grace" and discover a cliché in my writing?

You bet your sweet bippy.

THE GOOD VAMPIRE

Count Dracula:	"My dear, you have such a lovely neck. Dawn is coming soon. Give me a kiss."
She:	"Not on my life, baby !"

My company's president announced that he was looking for a volunteer to supervise the Red Cross blood drive held annually. I was a frequent blood donor when in the army and agreed to take the assignment after asking for a modest budget that he approved for committee lunches, printing, publicity, small prizes, and other odds and ends.

We formed a committee and set dates for a blood drive, determined to make this a fun project. It worked. After a few successful drives, we were collecting hundreds of pints of blood four times a year. The Columbus Red Cross blood bank was delighted and asked me to serve on their board. I accepted, and began learning the inner workings of a blood bank: blood processing, staffing, blood drives, public relations, and especially the relationship of our local chapter with the national Red Cross.

After a year, I was elected Chairman of the Columbus Board. The position required that I go to Washington several times a year to meet with the national board and staff.

The blood services wing of the Red Cross was at that time entirely separate from their relief and rescue activities. Elizabeth Dole had taken over the leadership of the blood services program and had initiated a management control tool she called The Transformation, a management program to centralize authority in the national office in Washington rather than at hundreds of local blood chapters all over the country.

Collecting blood from volunteer donors is a massive national operation, with more than fifteen million pints collected annually. To assure the safety of the blood supply, the Food and Drug Administration had the authority to close down a site if it was not proven reliable.

After blood is collected and processed locally, the blood is typically sold to more than two thousand local hospitals at more than thirty dollars per pint. Millions of dollars are involved, and no standard accounting practices were previously used, nor were quality control practices standardized, which occasionally caused quality control problems. FDA inspections frequently found sloppy bookkeeping. Some chapters were reliable, others ineffective and not well managed.

Local chapters had been independent for decades and fought to keep Washington out of their hair. The old argument over decentralization versus centralization in large organizations created immense tensions throughout the national system. Local chapters relied on volunteers to donate blood and sit on volunteer boards. Attempts to corral volunteer actions by a Washington bureaucracy caused very disgruntled reactions throughout the country.

Dole had her hands full. The Transformation, which was supervised by a retired general, sought to gain control of all finances, including bank accounts, personnel, blood processing procedures, contracts with local hospitals, administrative procedures, etc. Grumpy chapters were told that the Food and Drug Administration had demanded tighter controls or the entire blood services would be shut down. (The Red Cross supplies about 40 percent of all blood collected in the United States. If blood banks were shuttered, many people who needed blood would die.)

Ohio had eight or more local chapters, and the chapter chairmen and chairwomen met several times a year to talk things over. We were part of the larger Midwest Region, reaching from Michigan to West Virginia. Within a year I became the Ohio representative and Chair of the Midwest Region Board located in Detroit in a new modern building in the heart of the slums. That meant more travel, meetings, and angst about The Transformation.

Slowly, Dole and her hired general prevailed, and Red Cross Blood Services management was centralized in Washington. Fortunately, the Columbus chapter was supervised by a compliant, competent paid manager, Dr. Eng. With his leadership, we met all the demands of the national office, and we became a model site as well as one of its important cash cows.

Elizabeth Dole visited Columbus only once. The public affairs office managed her visit, featuring cocktail parties at downtown hotels with the press snapping photos and brief speeches here and there during which Mrs. Dole thanked volunteers and employees for our great results. It was a photo op, not serious interaction.

I am quick to relate that I was never a close buddy of Mrs. Dole nor her hubby. I was never invited for cocktails in their apartment at the Watergate.

Shortly thereafter I had a stroke. But my term of office was almost completed, and my participation with the Red Cross had begun to taper off.

Did my time volunteering with the Red Cross have any lasting effects? I can think of three important results. We started the first stem cell bank in Ohio with the cooperation of the Ohio State University, bankrolled by a $250,000 grant from the Ross Family Trust. We helped speed the completion of the dreaded but necessary Transformation. The blood drives I initiated continue in 2014.

And now a message for Count Dracula: Take your bloodletting elsewhere. You don't meet FDA standards.

ANTIQUES

By tradition, an antique is one hundred years old. That means that this year everything older than 1914 is authentically an antique. I do not qualify—*yet*.

Country Auctions

Living in the middle of rural Perry County thirty miles east of Columbus, Ohio, we discovered a new form of entertainment and a useful activity. We moved into our hundred-year-old farmhouse with a truckload of used furniture, castoffs donated by friends. Because the farmhouse was a weekend retreat, we never had any pretensions about classy digs. However, the Saturday farm auctions gave us a fine excuse to bid on, and buy antiques for the house.

Arriving at an auction site, we grazed the property for things we might like to buy, things like cherry end tables, dry sinks, pie safes, antique tools for decoration, Jerome shelf clocks, etc., all dating from the late 1800s farmhouses. Eventually we had a house full of attractive country antiques, most not quite one hundred years old.

Many of the sellers had purchased their goods from the Sears Roebuck catalogue. Pressed oak furniture was very popular, but we never liked it, preferring to buy things made of solid cherry, maple, or black walnut. Prices were cheap, and we hauled our finds home to decide whether the finish needed to be restored.

Antique Malls, Antique Stores, and Flea Markets

Having become addicted to antiques, we discovered that most cities and towns have antique malls or stores where dealers rent space to offer their wares.

I often browsed in them with no objective in mind. One exception was looking for Heisey glass. Marian and I received several wedding gifts of Heisey in 1955, and we started collecting berry bowls made prior to 1915. In all, we collected thirty and eventually donated them to the Heisey Museum in Newark, Ohio.

Other collections never amounted to much. One country auction featured dozens of American-made stemmed goblets manufactured in the 1800s. We bought a dozen. We also collected glass insulators that came in many colors and shapes. We had dozens of them but never coveted them as we did our Heisey glass.

Roaming flea markets became cheap weekend entertainment in Ohio and on a trip to England. In Keswick in the Lake Country, we bought six very small glass tumblers and a clear glass diamond optic bowl with attached amber feet. They sat in our dining room for years and became the vehicle for small drafts of single malt whiskey after meals.

Don and Jane Noyes and Pre–Antique Carving

Marian and I were befriended by Don and Jane Noyes. After retiring as a teacher, Don made his living dealing in antiques and working at local auctions. Our friendship was more personal. Don owned the woods north of our farm, and we sometimes needed to talk about cutting down lumber on our boundaries.

Later when we became interested in the American Arts and Crafts movement, Don began helping us find furniture made early in the 1900s. The first arts and crafts settle (couch) we bought was something Don found for us. It was not by Gustav Stickley, so we eventually donated the couch to the Thurber House Museum in Columbus, Ohio.

Don and Jane lived in a beautiful house in the woods north of Glenford, but they itched to convert their old barn downhill into a house. We watched the old derelict barn turn into a magnificent, grandiose home filled with carefully collected turn-of-the-century country artifacts.

Both Don and Jane enjoyed Pennsylvania Dutch bird trees. Don started carving similar ones, and Jane painted them. The results were extraordinary, and a new business grew as they became nationally know craftsmen. Their reputation grew to the extent that they were asked one year to carve a bird for one of the White House Christmas trees.

Jane had a gift for hooking imaginative rugs. She was known locally as one of Glenford's most famous hookers. We treasure the many meals we shared either in our restored bank or in their lovely barn.

The Arts and Crafts Movement: 1900–1920

Our 1920s bank in Glenford was an architectural anomaly. It was neoclassical on the outside, reflecting the Dulwich Gallery near London, England, but Arts and Crafts in the interior.

We were smitten with the idea of filling the bank with period pieces, both real and unreal. We bought books to study, and we haunted auctions and antique malls searching for gems: furniture, pottery, art, books, cloth, lamps, and anything else that was in that period style. We traveled twice to the annual Arts and Crafts convention where scholars, dealers, and collectors met at the Grove Park Inn in Ashville, North Carolina, to discuss the latest research and finds from across America. The result was successful enough to warrant an illustrated article about our bank in *Columbus Monthly*.

Reproduction and Fake Antiques

Often authentic antiques were completely out of our price range. For example, the real L. and J. G. Stickley Arts and Crafts prairie settle I wanted was valued at $64,000 and sold to Malcolm Forbes. Instead we bought a wonderful reproduction from the L. and J. G. Stickley (0wned by Audi) catalogue for $4,000. Its quality was higher than the original.

But I sinned in many ways. I purchased a Stickley round table at auction, the same table once located in Gustav's daughter's bedroom at the Craftsman Farms. But lo, it had been refinished, making it almost worthless. (Never, never restore an antique, no matter how bad it looks.)

Many fake antiques masquerade as real. In a small antique shop in Tel Aviv, the store owner brought out a cigar box filled with small metal daggers, and hatchets he said were from Luristan (Western Iran) and six thousand years old. They looked old. Pitted and dirty. I fell immediately and bought six examples for eleven dollars each. Oh, how I wanted them to be real. Years later, tramping through the British Museum, I found an exact replica of my hatchet head. Could it be? Probably not.

Fakers have become masterful at reproducing ancient metal and pottery by burying them outdoors for decades to acquire the correct patina. I was probably duped, but I loved the possibilities offered in that little Israeli store.

The Future

In 2029 I will officially become an antique.

Where will you be?

GAMES WE PLAY

A deck of cards is a practical gift for young children. The games they play help them learn their numbers without a teacher or parent lurking over them. The most childish card game is called War, which was probably the first game I ever learned. Remember? Turn cards over. The player with the highest card takes them both, puts both on the bottom of his stack. The game is over when one side has all the cards.

Before and after dinner in the summer months when I was a boy, we played street games. Hide-and-seek was the most common. You learned all the hiding spots so that when you were IT you could find your quarry easily. When bored with hide-and-seek, we played Red Rover or a game in which someone would throw a ball in the air, call a chum's name, and that person would try to catch the ball before the ball fell to the ground. The most inane game was Statues. Each of us would spin around until dizzy. When someone called "Stop," each participant froze in a grotesque pose, the uglier the better.

Laundry lines were used for skipping rope, and Double Dutch required the most skill.

We played ground games: jacks, marbles, flipping cards that came from bubble gum packages. We carried penknives and played a game in which a square was inscribed in the dirt. Contestants threw their knives into the dirt. Where the blade landed determined which part of the square would be eliminated until no space remained, and the game ended.

On rainy days, board games were unpacked: checkers, parcheesi, Monopoly, dominoes, old maids, Chinese checkers, tiddlywinks, and others.

In fair weather, we played lawn games, notably badminton and croquet.

My brothers were athletic. They played football, wrestled, and in the spring threw the shot put. I was the scrawny little brother. I weighed 129 pounds when I was married and was too small and skinny to play contact sports in school. I was the football manager and a coxswain on the JV crew in college. I played a little golf as a teenager, but never as an adult.

After my dad died, my mother and I played pinochle with neighbors at least once a week. Marian and I were taught bridge by a wonderful elderly couple, the Mankers. Both Mr. and Mrs. Manker were expert players but had the patience to teach novices, as we were. After playing several full games, Mr. Manker tore up the score sheet while Mrs. Manker went to the kitchen to cut large pieces of her delicious apple pie for a postgame treat.

When we bought a home computer, its games entertained me, and still do. We bought a Hoyle CD and dabbled in many card games. Today's favorites are bridge, solitaire, and gin. I spend hours playing Mahjong, Snood,

Bookworm, and Text Twist. These mindless games qualify as tranquilizers for the elderly.

Now it's your turn to play.

You're IT.

Government as
Theater (2013)

Hoopla has always been a part of politics: banners, torchlight parades, over-the-top oratory, scandal, and humbug. Now, however, politics has become virtual, phony, fake, and unreal. Things are done for effect, not substance. Politicians become robots, managed by "experts," handlers, and pollsters.

Why does Obama use a TV prompter? To be sure he stays on message. Speeches are delivered in locations selected to reinforce the message on sets designed with a proper look. Job growth speeches, for example, are typically made at a manufacturing site. Nothing is left to chance. The audience is carefully selected to reflect the message. If the theme is the future, the speech is made in a high school or college. All racial groups are calculated and placed where the camera will see them.

Focus groups test and retest the messages that have been selected by the White House staff. The president becomes the deliverer-in-chief. Afterward, polls are conducted to evaluate the impact. The pollsters analyze all relevant demographics: red states, blue states, men, women, young, old, blacks, Latinos, right-handed, left-handed. Who knows how many subgroups are analyzed.

Political campaigns are even more theatrical. Opposition research is conducted to discover everything negative about the opposing candidate. The resulting findings are made into TV and print ads that deflate the opposing candidate using the worst photos or film to make a candidate look horrible. Music is selected to sound ominous. Both parties use the same techniques. Millions are spent on TV ads, one side trying to outspend the other. The sources of the money are often unknown.

Even telephone solicitations are prerecorded for message control and efficiency. Political direct mail is sent under the letterhead of Robert Redford or Jimmy Carter to impress the recipient.

Candidates for high office are carefully vetted. No financial hanky-panky is tolerated, no juicy sexual affairs (especially after Clinton), no nefarious habits nor skeletons in the closet. Communication experts create a narrative for important candidates with paid flacks placing articles, interviews, and editorials in important media until the virtual, pure candidate becomes the person who has been imagined.

Congressional committees hold hearings that are scripted so that both political parties can put forward their positions. I recently spent several hours watching the oversight hearings on the rollout of the Obamacare website. Democrats lobbed softball questions at the witnesses. Republicans asked questions to embarrass them. There were no exceptions that I heard. Hours went by, completely predictable. Politics has become show business.

When a person is chosen for high office, he or she is surrounded by a horde of solicitous people responding willingly to requests, orders, even demands. Office holders begin to think of themselves as the king of the roost, and they are. Their egos swell, and they lose their human identities.

Where I worked I saw the phenomenon often. If a normal person was elected CEO by a board of directors, that person suddenly became petulant, demanding, and overbearing. Limos, private planes, unlimited expense accounts, and sycophants are not good for the soul.

Alas poor Barack, I knew him well.

Poignant Moments Recently

Last night Marian went to bed at ten thirty, and I came in at eleven. Marian stirred.

MARIAN: Do you miss your wife?

TOM: (Thinking fast) Do you mean the old Marian?

MARIAN: Yes.

TOM: We are in our mid-eighties. We're lucky to be alive.

End of conversation. And so it goes.

I first noted Marian's dementia on October 9, 2009. She wandered out into the hallway, returned, and said, "That's not the bathroom."

On December 8, 2013, Marian said to me, "I am falling apart."

Nuts to You

During childhood, several beloved treats would appear at the holiday season. A bowl of tangerines and a bowl of mixed nuts, still in their shells, were placed in the living room. A nutcracker sat on top of the nuts—not a fanciful nutcracker, but a plain metal one hinged at one end. My problem? Which nut to select before the rest of the family gobbled their favorites.

Among the selection were almonds, filberts, English walnuts, pecans, and Brazil nuts. My choice was almonds, and I recall sitting by the bowl cracking and eating one after another until there were none. The Brazil nuts were the last to go because they were so hard to crack. The holiday collection contained no peanuts, but Mother provided a separate bowl of roasted peanuts in the shell.

Some nuts are difficult to crack. (Where do you think the phrase "a hard nut to crack" came from?) English walnuts the size of golf balls are difficult to crack, as are the filberts, Brazil nuts, and pecans. Peanuts are easy, and with experience you can pop them open with your fingers in two perfect halves. But have you ever tried to crack a black walnut? *Do not try to crack a black walnut* without prior warning.

In the early forties, when I was twelve, I gathered a bushel basket of black walnuts from a tree near where we lived.

They were still in the thick, leathery green skin. We stored the nuts in the basement and began removing the outer shells. As I was paring off the peel, I noticed that my hands were turning rust red. *No matter,* I thought, *I will wash my hands when I am through.* Wrong. I washed and washed. My hands were stained red for months. Never, never pare the outer coat of black walnuts without wearing gloves.

Then came the hard part: cracking the black walnut shell. I tried the nutcracker without success. A hammer was required to crack the nuts. Even after the nut was splintered, it required a sharp metal pick to extract the meat in little shards. A sledgehammer would make a better nutcracker.

Today I buy roasted mixed nuts already shelled. The mixture contains a high percentage of peanuts, and they are the tastiest of all.

Breathes there the man with soul so dead who never to himself hath said, "Peanuts are one of God's great gifts." Is anything better than a peanut butter and jelly sandwich? Over a lifetime, I have added a variety of foods to peanut butter sandwiches: bacon, potato chips, raisins, mayonnaise, even Lebanon bologna.

I am nutty about peanuts and peanut butter.

Isn't everyone?

RESIDING N THE ARMS
OF MORPHEUS

We lose consciousness several times a day and night. It's called sleep. If we don't sleep, we become tired, lethargic, and grumpy. Many people have sleep problems and rely on drugs to fall asleep and stay asleep. Throughout my married life, I always had one serious problem: I snored loudly. So loudly that my wife complained for over fifty years. She tried everything to lessen the roar—putting her head under a pillow, prodding me awake, recording the noise to prove what a sonic boom I made. When I discussed the problem with my internist, she recommended sleeping with my head atop two pillows, which I tried to no avail.

Then one night Marian was lying awake listening to me breathe. She noted that every once in a while I stopped breathing. The longest pause was forty-five seconds. I mentioned this to my California internist, and he scheduled a sleep test at the Stanford University sleep lab.

On arrival, the tech placed wires all over my scalp and put me to bed. I worried that I wouldn't sleep and mess up the experiment, but apparently I did sleep. When I met with the attending physician, he said that I had sleep apnea and had stopped breathing through the night over fifty times. He prescribed a machine with a face mask to force air into my lungs during the night.

Bingo—my snoring was explained. From that time I stopped snoring if I had my mask on. The mask created one small new problem. It was very difficult to kiss Marian goodnight while wearing the mask, so we invented the air kiss with a few pats on the shoulder to say goodnight.

And no more snoring complaints.

SANA MENTE, SANUM CORPORE

The Latin slogan carved into the lintel of my high school was "Sound Mind in a Sound Body." Teachers and administrators were expected to produce educated kids who were healthy in mind and body.

However, one or the other quality always seemed to dominate—the athletes versus the bright kids. Very few had both qualities, but some did, for example, Jim Billington. He was the captain of our soccer team and our valedictorian—and the villain in our senior play. Jim was also valedictorian at Princeton and earned a doctorate at Oxford, then headed the Woodrow Wilson Institute at Princeton. Advisor to Ronald Reagan on Russian affairs, he became Librarian of the Congress in 1987. Jim obviously had a sound mind in a sound body. He is now eighty-six.

I am eighty-five, and things have changed. The mind becomes a bit forgetful, and the body is complaining. As I watch people age, I wonder whether a sound mind or a sound body is preferable. Either one has liabilities and advantages. Of course, we all desire both a sound mind in a sound body. Unfortunately, age brings problems with both. Sorry!

Wracked with Alzheimer's disease, Mother died a week before her ninetieth birthday, completely non compos mentis. Her former diseases, such as high blood pressure, had remitted, a common benefit in the demented.

Here is a hypothetical question: If you were required to select one, which would it be? Would you prefer a clear mind or a healthy body if you only have one choice? Don't answer too fast. I have asked many residents in our retirement community, and they usually answer "Sound mind." They believe being clearheaded is preferable to having a debilitating and perhaps painful disease. Sounds logical, doesn't it? Think again. Many demented folks don't realize they have lost their memory and reasoning power.

However, in the long run none of us have a choice. We cope with whatever happens.

Life's an unpredictable crapshoot.

WHERE IS THE DAMN CAR?

Every driver has had the experience of parking his or her car somewhere and not remembering where the damn thing is. Manufacturers understand the problem, because these days they provide a key fob with a button that, when pushed, will make the horn toot or the headlights flash. *Voila, le car.* Well, maybe.

Every summer, the Columbus Symphony Orchestra gave a series of outdoor concerts on the campus of Chemical Abstracts. Before the concert the orchestra sponsored a picnic-in-the-park featuring tables for ten and a potluck approach for the food. Our company bought one of the tables every year to support the orchestra, and employees signed up to go to the concert. Each family would be assigned to bring one course for ten people.

On this August evening, the theme was western. We all bought western shirts and bolo ties. Flowers were ordered for the table, an attractive wooden construction serving as a base for the cut flowers. As we arrived in our cars, a cadre of attendants guided us in tidy rows in the park to the rear of the building, under the trees. When we left the car, I noted that we were parked under a large oak tree that would serve as my beacon for car retrieval after the concert.

The evening passed pleasantly. The concert featured the Ohio State Marching Band as guest musicians. The concert ended with a rousing rendition of "Stars and Stripes Forever." The centerpiece at the table was awarded to Marian because her birthday fell closest to the date of the concert. I carried the heavy flower arrangement weighing, I estimate, ten pounds.

Then the trouble began. By now it was pitch-black, and there were no lights in the car park. The headlights of the leaving cars obscured my visibility as I searched for the oak tree under which we were located. I couldn't see *any* big oak tree. We were stranded, and the centerpiece I was carrying now seemed to weigh a ton.

We walked up and down the remaining rows of cars. Nothing. Could our car have been stolen? Panic. Then a strategy emerged. Let's wait until everyone leaves, and there will be our car. Bingo! It took over half an hour before our car appeared magically in the wilderness. I should have abandoned the heavy flowers, but I was too preoccupied to think of that.

Don't laugh. You have forgotten where you parked your car at least once or twice.

THE EYES HAVE IT

Have you ever noticed that some people have sleepy eyes? Their eyes droop (technically called ptosis) and are half-closed.

They might have diabetes. As diabetes progresses, the muscles in the eyelid sometimes begin to weaken, and the lids remain half-closed. That's what happened to me. A simple test revealed the extent of the problem. A tech asks you to stare at a black dot. She has a little light on the end of a pole that she moves around. "Tell me when you can see the light. Don't move your head," she says. The metrics revealed that my peripheral vision was shot.

"We will send you to our eyelid doctor," said the ophthalmologist. Can you believe that the Palo Alto Medical Foundation has a doctor who specializes in droopy eyelids? They do, and he is very nice. He explained that the eyelid surgery would be an outpatient procedure under local anesthetic.

I was awake during the operation, and I remember him saying, "Half-done." I'm glad he did the other half. I would look silly with one eye open and the other droopy. When we went outside into the sunlight, I discovered there was a sky up there and a pavement down there. When I looked into a mirror, I still had eyelashes, so he must have extracted skin from elsewhere on the lid.

Years earlier I was diagnosed with cataracts in both eyes. Night driving became difficult as oncoming lights flared, and daytime driving presented a brown haze over the landscape. After the initial diagnosis, we waited for the cataracts to "ripen."

(The word *ripen* reminds me of fruit. Do you remember the game we once played at Halloween parties where we passed fruit under a sheet, being told they were body parts? Dried pears were ears, Grapes were eyes. Very spooky!)

How many people develop cataracts? Statistics reveal that about half of people over forty. Fifty years ago removal was a major surgery, requiring the patient to lie still in bed for several weeks with his or her head supported by sand bags so the head could not move. Now cataract surgery is a routine, safe procedure, using a special instrument to suck out the cataract followed by a small incision in the eye for the implant of a lens that snaps in place after it is inserted. Glasses are prescribed to provide nearly normal, balanced vision. After the operation, the beneficial results are immediate. Brown haze turns to bright blue clarity. Night driving is possible without flare.

When I selected new glasses frames after the operation, I chose wire rims with oval, horizontal lenses. Then I discovered that John Lennon's similar frames were round.

Damn, I thought I was being so cool!

THE SWEATER FROM
THE ISLE OF IONA

In my mid-eighties, I am still impulse ridden. This is a VIN YET about a sweater I recently bought that I don't need. You may assume that I am now officially senile.

On a quiet afternoon in the mid-1960s, an elderly friend brought one of his friends to talk. The guest was Sir George MacLeod, a noted liberal theologian from Scotland. MacLeod was known as the founder of the Iona Community, a religious retreat and study center on the Isle of Iona, a tiny island off the west coast of Scotland. The medieval abbey there had fallen in disrepair and was restored as a project of the community. The history of the island dates to AD 586. The current abbey was originally constructed about AD 1200.

Iona is a wild, remote place, the burial place of forty-five Scandinavian kings, including Macbeth. Saint Columba, who lived there in the sixth century, is believed to have christianized Britain from this wee isolated island.

MacLeod invited me to visit the community on Iona at a future date, but he explained that only one bed and breakfast was available, and we needed to make reservations a year in advance. A year later my family and I made the trip.

A steamer ferry left Oban on the west coast of Scotland and sailed for the Isle of Mull. When the boat docked in Mull, we were met by a bus headed to the port where we could be transported to Iona. We bumped along for thirty-five miles to Fionnphort at the other end of Mull, where we transferred to an open, motorized, dinghy for the trip across the Sound of Iona.

The tiny village of Iona has only one lane along the beach, and about thirty stone houses and stores. Off in the distance stood the imposing, restored abbey and Iona Community center.

After breakfast we toured the abbey and the adjacent graveyard featuring elaborately carved Celtic crosses. The abbey, dating from the 1200s, is mostly unadorned and more famous for its illustrious history than for its bleak Romanesque architecture.

Iona is three miles long and half a mile wide, mostly undeveloped. The few shops featured local crafts. We shopped to buy something to remind us of the visit. One store featured hand-knit Aran fishermen's sweaters, made with handmade yarn in its natural color. I bought a sweater that fit me well. I wore it for years, and then I started to gain weight, and the sweater became too tight. It disappeared, but the memory lingered. I wanted another one.

The Internet reaches into eternity. Aran sweaters? Many websites and dozens of sweaters to buy. I could feel the impulses tugging in my brain. Buy, buy, buy! The best hand-knit sweaters cost nearly three hundred dollars. Too indulgent. But a machine-made sweater was a third of the price. Do it! Happiness a click away.

Remember my sizing problem and the weight gain, I hit upon a solution: buy a cardigan. It would fit no matter my size.

Aran sweaters provide great warmth, but this is California and the weather is mild. Why buy a heavy sweater? Because winter is here and chilly days call for a heavy sweater. Rationalize, rationalize. Click, the deed is done, the sweater is bought, and my memory transported back to Iona.

PS: Marian and I returned to Iona five years after our first visit. Not much had changed. Time marches on. I love my new sweater. It fits perfectly. Marian said, "I want one too."

We are hopelessly senile, but we love our new fisherman sweaters.

Peekaboo, I See You

The US government is mammoth, with about 4,200,000 employees. Thousands of the jobs are top secret, and the typical citizen has no idea what any of the people in those jobs accomplish.

Folks of my generation wonder, "How could the Germans let a madman like Hitler come to power?" The answer is lethargy and fear.

Hitler made scapegoats of the Jews to justify his paranoia and evil deeds. In our times, we are learning to fear and hate Muslims. Patterns of past history are reoccurring.

Because of Islamic terrorist activity, more and more of the federal budget is spent on surveillance. We learn that our government has developed meta-collection systems to collect phone records and access to e-mails from fifty major databases. The president assures us that no one is listening to individual phone calls or reading e-mails and that to protect us against terrorists, our privacy has been compromised just a little.

To listen to our calls or read our e-mail, approval must be authorized by a secret court. Who are the judges making decisions, and what are their political leanings? Note that defendants are not represented at the court. Only the government's side is heard.

We learn that our government has one hundred thousand private contractors with top-secret clearances. Who cleared them, and are they reliable? Probably not. When we buy something on line, most companies attach a cookie to our account enabling them recommend items we may want to buy. Our privacy is eroded every day because the Internet enables it.

I am not suspicious by nature, but I am sure that among the millions of government employees and contractors, there must be at least 150 people who don't care about my privacy. George Orwell in his ominous novel *1984*, published sixty-four years ago, described a government that snooped on all citizens. The government punished people they didn't like with the things they feared most—in my case, the IRS.

I am not paranoid enough to imagine that I am currently at personal risk. But I do sense a serious creep toward a more invasive government. Is Obama evil? Probably not, but all humans have a dark side, and I am reminded of President Nixon, who lied to us while claiming that he was not a crook.

Am I under investigation? When my wife and oldest daughter call one another, they may talk for forty-five minutes. Somewhere in Langley, Virginia, I can imagine a buzzer going off and a computer nerd hollering, "Hey, look at this."

We are experiencing surveillance creep, and it bothers me. We should all feel a bit queasy and worry about further privacy loss.

"Be afraid, be very afraid!"

THE CLOAK-AND-DAGGER GAME

When the nice little old lady next door peeks through her lace curtains to see who you are entertaining, that's called spying. Well, not quite, but almost. These days everyone is spying on everyone. The art has become a scientific bonanza for the software folks. Cloaks and daggers are out, computers are in. Well, not quite, but almost. Spies are still lurking in hotel bars all over the world, hiding messages under rocks, and sending coded texts to their handlers in every capitol in the world.

Spying is a natural human instinct. We all want to know what others are doing and thinking, even when it is none of our business. Now it is everyone's business. Buy anything on the Internet and soon you will receive a message: "You may also be interested in …" I learned that our computers are filled with cookies, little bits of messages that reveal our computer habits and activities. If you want to, you can de-cookie your computer, but I don't care if everyone knows that I bought a book last week about living aboard an aircraft carrier. But I am disturbed that Target and PayPal have been hacked. Now any hacker can trace my identity.

Spying has a long history, and spies are so common that a genre called "spy novels" exists. John Le Carré has earned millions churning out thrilling books that keep us reading. (So have Robert Ludlum and Tom Clancy.)

Secrets are wonderful. We want to be in the know. We all want to spy. Gossip nourishes our need to know, especially something that is supposed to be a secret. When a friend begins by saying, "Don't tell anyone I told you …" you immediately pay close attention and begin wondering who you will share this delicious tidbit with.

To be serious, spying has evolved from a primitive profession to a highly sophisticated art form that envelops every person, every government. After Sputnik was launched, we launched spy satellites to photograph troop movements, warship positions, and supply trucks taking centrifuges to atomic energy sites. However, we sometimes make mistakes. Weapons of mass destruction may appear in our minds, not in reality, and we go to war. A little knowledge is a dangerous thing.

Or a lot of knowledge. Edward Snowden has revealed that we are now collecting megadata on everything about everybody. Think about it. Billions are being spent by our government searching for clues of malfeasance. Because of lone-wolf behavior, everyone is potentially dangerous, not just those ominous Russians and the silly North Koreans. *Everyone !*We collect more and more and more intelligence.

We can react to threats in frightening ways. Drones can fly everywhere and launch heat-seeking guided missiles into a moving car. Oh, what glorious paranoia can do for the imagination. Think of all the things we can get rid of: noisy children, old men who talk too loud, dogs that bark at night. Create your own list and make a plan to attack.

Last week the Justice Department indicted five Chinese hackers who were spying on American companies to gather industrial intelligence. That's not new. All companies collect information on competitors, covertly and overtly. Computer companies are notorious for stealing one another's secrets, even by planting spies in workforces. Cyber warfare is a fact. Hacking is a profession. Hackers usually wear tee shirts, not trench coats or fedoras pulled down low over slinky eyes.

The Bill of Rights protects us against unlawful search and seizure. Or it used to. Now almost every branch of federal government has its own undercover spy agency—the Department of Justice, the Department of Defense, plus the CIA, the FBI, NSA, and too many others to name. Budgets are secret and disguised. Billions are spent, and all of us are in the web.

Fortunately, most agencies are incompetent, so we are protected, unless you are a Republican, in which case you have been declared an enemy of the people.

MY OLDER SIBLINGS:
THE TWINS, JACK AND JIM

My older brothers, the twins, were born in 1924. I was born in 1929. This fact was the basis for the nearly lifelong separation of our lives. When I was five, they were ten. When I was ten, they were fifteen. When I was fifteen, they were twenty. We lived in separate worlds.

We had other differences. They were short, stocky, genial, and hearty. I was skinny, taller, serious, and often sickly with frequent bouts of tonsillitis. They had their friends and playmates, and I had mine. They loved to roughhouse. I didn't. We were a cohesive family, but they lived in one world, and I lived in another. When they became teenagers, they became interested in sports: football, wrestling, and track. When I went to high school, I weighed 125 pounds and became the football team manager, not a player.

Their paternal grandmother could not tell them apart, they were that identical. When the twins were babies, Mother dressed them identically. When they went into the Army Air Corps, the policy was to keep twins together. They served together throughout their service.

They were identical in many ways. Often as they slept, I noticed that they were sleeping in identical positions, even though they were in separate twin beds. However, they had differing personalities. Jack was more placid and friendly. Jim was more intense, more inside himself. You might expect that the twins would be competitive, but that never seemed evident. They were two peas in a pod, doing things together, almost as one. They had a devilish streak, but when they got into trouble, never blamed the other. We will never know which one put his foot through the bedroom wall when roughhousing in their bedroom.

When they reached sixteen, Dad bought them a used car. They called it "The Green Hornet," a green Pontiac sedan with a governor set at thirty-five miles per hour. Their favorite pastime was finding the steepest hill they could to see how fast they could make the car go downhill.

They developed an interest in football and played opposite guard positions and were good enough to play on the first team in high school. In track they threw the shot put. They practiced in the front and back yards, which eventually had many divots. Jack was the better wrestler and competed in the high school state finals. For earning a little money as teenagers, they caddied at local golf courses.

They had huge appetites. After finishing a supper, they might open and eat a quart can of applesauce. Occasionally at the dinner table, they would holler, "Look at the submarine." When I looked up, one would try to take my pork chop. Mother would make the perpetrator give it back.

Health issues plagued them from their teenage years. Jack had high blood pressure issues before he was twenty. Jim suffered from eczema for years. Dad bought an ultraviolet lamp, and Jim had ten minutes exposure every day for a decade. Both the twins died in their early forties, as Dad had. Jack died first of a massive stroke, even though he was under the medical care of a professor at the University of Pennsylvania.

They both went to and graduated from the Wharton School of Business at the University of Pennsylvania. Jack went to work for A. O. Smith selling glass-fused silos. Jim, on the other hand, had larger plans. After working for Mother's sister's family as a salesman, he started his own operation selling chemical megasupplies to clients. For example, he sold carloads of salt to the Pennsylvania Highway Department. All for naught. Genetics did them in.

Did I have a favorite? Yes. Jack played the role of my protector. When I sought comfort, he would let me crawl in bed beside him. We were good friends. He looked out for me.

When they returned from the Air Corps, they completed college and soon married. As adults we interacted infrequently. I have a feeling of guilt that we were not closer. They had a twinkling sense of humor, were good natured and always on the go.

Among the kin they were known as the "twinnies." Our Dad was exceedingly proud of them. Mother worried they would get hurt playing football.

I was always the little brother.

Honey, I'm Home

This morning I read the following from an article in the *New York Times*.

In the first joint result from the world's two leading particle colliders, scientists have determined the mass of the heaviest elementary particle, the top quark.

"The measurement was made using the Large Hadron Collider (LHC) at CERN in Geneva, Switzerland, and the Tevetron at Fermilab in Batavia, Ill. Four separate experiments found a joint value for the top quark of 173.34 (+/- O.76) gigaelectrovolts divided by the speed of light squared, scientists announced Wednesday (March 19) at a physics conference in Italy.

The four LHC and Tevatron experiments—ATLAS, CDP, CMS, and DZERO, respectively—are the only ones that have observed top quarks, which are 100 times the mass of a proton. In addition to top quarks, there are five other types, or flavors of quarks: bottom, up, down, charm, and strange. (For instance, protons are made of two up quarks and one down quark, whereas neutrons contain two down quarks and one up quark.)

I'll be damned. Who would have thought it? I am thrilled but befuddled. What is a gigaelectrovolt? How will I recognize a charm quark when I meet one? I am disappointed too. I thought when they identified the Higgs boson, the physicists had solved all of cosmology with nothing left to learn. Oh well.

"Honey, I'm home."

"Did you stop at the collider and bring any charming or strange quarks home for supper?"

"No, they didn't look ripe."

"It doesn't matter, I made lasagna."

Physics and physicists confuse me. My physics course in college wasn't so much about mathematics as experiments with wire boards, slide rules, and flow charts. Now cartoons about physics normally show blackboards with elaborate formulae on them with experts debating a plus or a minus sign. Obviously I have been left way behind, never to learn the secrets of it all.

For example, what the hell *is* a gigaelectrovolt? Don't tell me. I don't want to know. I now am suspicious that the CIA hires all the physicists to spy on me.

Please, I am eighty-five, and I am innocent.

I Ain't Sick, Yet

In the middle of December 2013, I had a fainting spell. The day before and the day after fainting, I experienced twenty minutes of serious dizziness. After six hours in the hospital, I was discharged because they couldn't find anything wrong, but daughter Janice and her husband Mark, both experienced nurses, tentatively diagnosed my malady as ventricular tachycardia. A search began to find out what was going on. My internist referred me to a cardiologist.

The cardiologist took my history and ordered a series of tests that went on for four months. "We know what happened, but we don't know why it happened," he opined. Neither did I, and I hoped that advanced medical technology would figure it out.

What fools we mortals be.

I may not have the recommended tests in proper sequence, but it was something like this: electrocardiogram, heart and carotid doppler, two-day Holter, then a twenty-eight-day Holter. When the results of all those tests were inconclusive, the cardiologist ordered a chemical stress test. That test was not revealing.

I was becoming more convinced by the day that medical practice was a costly bunch of hooey. Months were passing by. Was I sick or wasn't I? My psyche required an answer. A bit of fibrillation was detected, but not enough to do anything about. Janice and Mark called the cardiologist to learn the fine details of the tests, which had producing medical gobbledygook that baffled me.

Was I sick? Or wasn't I sick? Heaven only knows. The tests probably cost over $5,000 at that point.

But the big test was yet to come, the Diagnostic Cardiac Electrophysiology Study. This test costs in the neighborhood of $10,000 and requires hospitalization "but is perfectly safe," the electrocardiologist assured me. "We enter the groin and string a wire into your heart. Then we try to induce fibrillation. If you fibrillate and won't come out of it, we will have to shock you. That could be uncomfortable." Whoopee, that's exciting and very reassuring!

On the appointed day, I woke at four to be sure I had time get up, dress, eat something if my blood sugar was low, and meet my driver at five thirty. My blood sugar was low—71, and I was feeling hypoglycemic. So I ate a ham and cheese croissant and a small can of V8 juice. (I had earlier called Dr. Levy's office nurse to discuss the diabetes problem. She never told me I *must not eat anything* after midnight.) When I was in the prep room, Dr. Levy came in and said he learned that I had eaten an hour before. "We either have to cancel, or do the operation without sedation. Your choice."

I asked about pain level. (I am a coward.) "None, if everything goes well. I will numb where we put the electrode in your groin. Otherwise, no pain." By now I was irritated with the entire test phase and wanted to get things over ASAP, so I told him we would proceed without sedation.

When we entered to operating room, all four gowned, masked people were in a happy mood. They noted the tattoo on my shoulder, and we discussed how and when I got it. (Answer: when I was eighty, as a birthday gift from my daughter.)

I could not recognize Dr. Levy and asked whether he was there. "No, he's in an anteroom waiting for us to have you ready," I was told. I had wires running everywhere, and the monitors were checked to see whether my heart was beating. Scotty put a cup over my naked genitals "to complete the illusion of modesty." One nurse to my left was staring at my groin. I tried to be nonchalant.

A few minutes later, Dr. Levy entered, and the procedure proceeded. The only pain I felt was the entrance of the numbing needle, followed by a bit of tugging as he threaded the wire into my heart.

This test takes one and a half hours. All the while the nurse at my left was staring at my groin. presumably to watch my incision. In a while Dr. Levy moved to the side of the room to an array of equipment and the fun began. I could hear clicking, and my heart started thumping—all expected and normal. Finally it was over. Dr. Levy leaned over me and said, "You passed with flying colors." (Note the use of a well-worn, Pollyanna cliché.)

After this procedure it is necessary to have bed rest for four hours. When I arrived in the recovery room, the chart board noted bed rest for six hours. *Damn.* I had told the driver I would be ready to go home at noon. Now discharge could take place after the drivers would be going home. I started to sulk and plan escape. But being sweet and complacent, I just lay there getting madder. Some food was brought in, but I was warned not to raise my head. Did you ever try to eat and drink flat on your back? Not easy.

The next day I was scheduled to see my regular cardiologist to learn the details of the test and to plan a strategy of therapy. "I haven't heard from Dr. Levy," my cardiologist said. "If anything bad happened, he would have called me." I was fuming mad and told him so. Nearly four months had gone by, probably $20,000 or more of tests, and we are back to square one. No therapy was recommended. I am now officially "under observation."

I ain't sick, yet. But I am frustrated as hell.

A CAT'S AFFECTION

Our cat Tillie is very affectionate.
He comes close and rubs against my leg.
Then he steps back and sits on his haunches,
Staring at me with a tender stare.
Love me please, his eyes plead.
I want to be your friend.
When I don't respond, he reaches up
and pets my knee. I rub his chin.
Does he love me?
No, he wants to be fed.

I Love Coffee, I Love Tea ...

I love coffee, I love tea
I love the java jive, and it loves me
Coffee and tea and the java and me
A cup, a cup, a cup, a cup, a cup

—The Ink Spots, 1940

People fit into one of two categories. They are either tea drinkers or coffee drinkers. Either way, both beverages are surrounded by long histories, both personal and historic. Tea is by far the most popular drink globally, but coffee is more associated with America, the typical morning wake-up beverage. (Of course, water is the most widely consumed fluid.)

As a child, coffee was reserved for adults. On very special occasions, Mother would stir a few teaspoons of coffee into a glass of milk as a treat. I didn't think so. I would have preferred chocolate syrup in my milk. Coffee made things bitter. Mother frequently made cocoa or hot tea for me in the morning—Lipton tea in a teabag. I would dip my buttered toast into the sweetened tea as one of my morning rituals.

Tea was nothing special until I started traveling abroad, when I learned that many kinds of tea existed. Wandering the streets in Geneva, I located a store selling nothing but teas and tea paraphernalia. I bought six or seven varieties of tea as souvenirs and began experimenting with differing styles and flavors: green teas, jasmine flavored, smoked teas, and others. In England we drank Earl Grey flavored with bergamot and at home a brand called Constant Comment flavored with orange peel. Today I drink iced tea with lemon at lunch and dinner. I don't drink coffee at all anymore, even though for most of my married life, we brewed coffee every morning.

Like beer, coffee is an acquired taste. I never drank coffee until my army days, when hot coffee was always available. In Germany on bivouac after it snowed, we spent hours standing around the mess tent holding steaming cups of coffee in metal canteens, keeping our hands warm.

While in the army, I took a trip to Italy, asked for coffee, and was served dynamite in a tiny cup. What was that? Espresso, of course. Talk about an acquired taste! After trying more I began to like it very much. The Abbott office in Geneva had a small kitchenette with an espresso maker, and I would drink three or four cups a day when I was there. We bought an espresso maker for our home in Ohio and served espresso in small cups I bought in Germany.

Two countries grew coffee I especially liked, Kenya and Guatemala. I shipped seventeen pounds of beans home from Nairobi and stashed my suitcases full of coffee beans I bought at the airport in Guatemala. The Kenyan coffee was rich, with chocolate overtones. The Guatemalan coffee was mellow and comforting, The most exotic coffee I ever drank was in a Druze community near Haifa as the guest of a sheik. It was thick, deadly sweet, and laced with cardamom.

Coffee-making techniques vary widely: drip makers, French presses, percolators, espresso machines, etc. But at our weekend farm we brewed camp coffee—that is, we put ground coffee into boiling water, let it steep, and pour into mugs through a strainer.

When first learning to drink coffee, I used cream and sugar, or one of them. Eventually, I only drank it black.

Coffee cost ten cents a cup when I was boy. Now at Starbucks a cup might cost six dollars, but you can sit there all day writing the great American novel on your laptop.

The price is right!

WAR AND PIECES

Some say that Leo Tolstoy was a saint. Some say he was the world's finest novelist. Some say he was loony. He was all those things and more. Born in 1828 to a rich Russian family, he eventually denied all material things. He became a devout, converted Christian who condemned the legitimacy of the organized church and his Tsarist government. He became an enemy of both. Tolstoy disapproved of warfare. He preached nonviolent resistance, a philosophy that directly influenced Gandhi and Martin Luther King.

War and Peace

My exploration of Tolstoy began with an interest in his famous books. When sent to basic training in Camp Cooke, California, I bought a copy of *War and Peace* and kept it under my tunic. I read a page or two during ten-minute breaks, and at night and on weekends. The book is said to have 350 characters. My problem was learning to pronounce and remember all those Russian names. I would say them out loud phonetically, hoping my pronunciation was close.

Tolstoy's knowledge of the world was immense. For example, his battle scenes were a revelation, providing insight into battle planning, battle execution, and realistic portrayal of the battles. *War and Peace* was life changing. I promptly read more Tolstoy fiction.

The Kruetzer Sonata

The plot of this short novella is simple enough: a man and a woman fall in love after meeting by chance but have a very stormy and unpleasant marriage. The wife, a pianist, falls in love with a violinist, and they play Beethoven's "Kreutzer Sonata" together and begin a torrid love affair. The husband finds them in bed, and he murders her, jamming a dagger through her corset.

Tolstoy's novella, when read by a naïve twenty-year-old soldier stationed in Germany, knocked his socks off, amazed that a well-written book could evoke such intense, vivid emotion.

The Kingdom of God Is Within You

After becoming a world-famous novelist, Tolstoy had a deeply religious experience when he witnessed a brutal execution. He then became both a social philosopher and a serious critic of the Eastern Orthodox religion and his Tsarist government. He sought to be Christlike, ministering to the sick and impoverished peasants, denying materialism. In this important nonfiction book, he proposed nonviolent resistance to all forms of hostility and evil. He became an aesthete, denying his family and possessions.

I was at the time active in the Presbyterian Church: a deacon, an elder, clerk of session, Sunday school teacher of both adults and teenagers, choir member, etc. After reading *The Kingdom of God Is Within You*, I realized that the religion I knew had strayed far from the simplicity of Tolstoy's faith.

Tolstoy came to a sad end. At ninety-two, the old feeble man left his home to go on a "mission. He contracted pneumonia and was found by a stationmaster who took him in. He died in 1910.

Tolstoy's life as one of the world's greatest, most famous authors took a sudden turn late in his life. He personally communicated with Gandhi, who eventually took down Britain's domination of the world using a nonviolent resistance strategy. His writings led Martin Luther King to confront racism in the United States. Leo Tolstoy was a giant whose influence is still being felt. Think of Pope Francis and his recent pronouncements about income redistribution. Tolstoy would have approved.

STEAK

Mother fried steak for dinner occasionally. The butcher would cut a slab of bottom-of-the-round about a half inch thick. At dinnertime she would put the meat in a very hot cast-iron skillet, leaving it on the stove while she mashed the potatoes and opened a can of peas. After about fifteen minutes, she would flip the meat to cook on the second side. When eaten, the steak was charred and grey on the inside, tough and flavored with nothing. It never occurred to me that steak was supposed be a treat.

When drafted during the Korean war, I was dispatched to Camp Cook, which is near Lompoc, California. When we were granted passes on weekends, six of us would go into town for a restaurant meal. Most would order a steak, rare. *Rare!* How might that taste? In a fit of camaraderie, I too ordered rare. Blood ran on the plate when it came. *Ugh!* Then the first taste: sweet, soft, and chewable, bathed in a delicious sauce. Good Lord, what had I been missing? Rare was really good.

Yes, I have had beef that was too rare, so I usually order medium rare. And yes, I have tried *carpaccio,* but I prefer my meat cooked.

When we moved to the farm in 1961, I started grilling outside on weekends. I would go to the country store on Saturday morning and ask Luke Swinehart to cut one-inch-thick T-bone steaks. Slowly I learned how to cook them properly: seared on the outside, and medium rare on the inside. Sometimes I would sprinkle a bit of garlic powder before taking them off the grill, but I preferred only salt, pepper, and a big pat of butter to enrich the juices. A baked potato and corn on the cob with the steak became the ultimate summer feast.

Over the passing years, I have eaten many cuts of steak served many ways. In the stockyards in Omaha, Nebraska, I enjoyed aged beef. Aficionados of steak have favorites: rib eye, New York strip, flank, T-bone and filet mignon, for example. I have no particular favorite, but my heart leaps up when I anticipate a medium-rare filet laced with butter or a rich demi-glace. Even as succulent as filet may be, it seems to be enhanced by being dressed up a bit. A wrap of bacon adds almost too much flavor, but a dollop of caramelized onions can be heavenly. Steak-au-poire is an interesting variant. Thickness is also an issue—how much is enough? One inch, two inches? Once, thicker was better. Now, smaller is preferable, but the degree of rareness is the primary requirement.

Sides embellish the meat. Mashed potatoes and a few stalks of buttered asparagus are perfect.

I do not want to disparage my mother's cooking, even though her recipe for fried steak was grotesque. She did make a hell of a fine pot roast.

Thou Shall Not Eat French Fries

Stand back. Look out. Here comes a diatribe. I need to get this off my chest. I need to vent.

Let me introduce you to an author you probably don't know, Bertram Gross. According to his Wikipedia entry, in the 1960s he joined the faculty of Syracuse University in the Maxwell School of Business. In 1961–62, he was a Fellow at the Center for Advanced Study in the Behavioral Sciences, Palo Alto; and, in 1962–63, he was the Leatherbee Lecturer at the Harvard Business School. From 1970 to 1982, he was Distinguished Professor of Political Science and Urban Affairs at Hunter College and the CUNY Graduate Center.

In short, he has good credentials as a pundit. In 1980, Gross published a perceptive book entitled *Friendly Fascism*. In it he predicts the likelihood of an emerging totalitarian state imposed by the power elites in the government and corporate worlds based on friendly persuasion.

Don't leave me, I'm only getting started.

Don't focus on the word *fascism*. Focus on the word *friendly,* or you won't understand. *Friendly Fascism* proposes, "We need to manipulate you because we want to protect your well being. We need to help you. We make rules, regulations, products, and services because we have your interest at heart."

For example:

You must wear a helmet if you ride a bike or a motorcycle to protect you from concussion. Seat belts are required by law in case of a crash. Lives will be saved.

You shouldn't drink a large soda pop because it contains too much sugar. Therefore, we are outlawing sugary drinks larger than sixteen ounces (as they briefly did in New York City).

You can't smoke a cigarette indoors or outdoors. We are protecting your fellow humans from lung cancer.

We want to save you from harming yourself. Don't eat too much red meat. We are eliminating pizza and potatoes in school lunches. The children are too obese.

It all makes sense, doesn't it? No, it doesn't. The nanny state creeps on in a thousand ways, and we all succumb without a fight because we are being looked after. No Brownshirts or Storm Troopers are needed to keep us in line because most citizens are grateful for this fatherly advice that saves us from ourselves. I'm deeply concerned.

This diatribe is neither liberal nor conservative. Republicans and Democrats are equally culpable. Give politicians an inch, and they will regulate how you should measure that inch.

Do the prohibitions work?

Henry Marsh, who works at St. George's Hospital in London, said that many of his patients who have been in bike accidents have been wearing helmets that are too flimsy to be beneficial.

He cited evidence from the University of Bath that suggests that wearing a helmet may even put cyclists at greater risk. The research showed that drivers get three inches closer to cyclists who wear helmets because they perceive them as safer. Does no one understand the law of unintended consequences?

I am glad the government and corporations want to look out for me. But, instead of prohibitions, educate me, don't regulate me. Say, "We suggest that ..." and not "You must ... or else." Persuade me that greasy french fries may clog my arteries. Don't remove potatoes from the federal lunch program. Michelle Obama has good intentions, but ...

Little by little, inch by inch, our lives are being managed by others. Contemporary fascism is friendly. It attempts to make me live forever.

How can I influence this surreptitious, intrusive beast? The answer: Be brave. Ignore all those feel-good rules. Ride your bike without a helmet, enjoy your cheeseburger with bacon, agree to supersize your fries. Our early death will help solve the overpopulation problem.

Bertram Gross predicted this alarming trend thirty-five years ago. We all enjoy being coddled, but please don't try to protect me from myself.

I ate salty, greasy potato chips for lunch last week. Wow, were they good—for my psyche.

SUGGESTIONS FROM FRIENDS

Sometimes a chance remark by a friend can be life changing. For example, Don Doty once asked me whether I watched *CBS Sunday Morning*. He recommended the TV show enthusiastically. The next Sunday I watched and have been watching for the last thirty years. The program is aired at six AM in California, and I wake up at six, curl up on the couch with a warm robe over me, and enjoy this weekly TV magazine. Don never knew how much his suggestion meant to me over the years.

The president of Ross Labs, Dick Ross, knew I enjoyed art and classical music. He would stop my office to chat. "Tom, do you have a CD player? You would enjoy the convenience and sound quality. You can hear the entire Beethoven's Ninth on one CD." That week I bought a new sound system with a CD player. When I set it up, it didn't make a sound. I had put the CD in upside down. Only when out of frustration I turned the CD over did the beautiful music burst forth.

Later Dick told me that everyone should own a Volkswagen once in their lifetime. Volkswagens were new to the market in the fifties. The next car I bought was a blue Bug. The sale included a free maintenance program. The mechanics wore white coats, making a trip to the garage an occasion.

Finally, when Dick traveled to London, he often stayed at 11 Cadogan Gardens near Sloane Square. Later, on a trip with Barb and Steve Borik, we stayed in this elegant boutique hotel. If it was good enough for a company president, it was good enough for us.

Phil Greth was an adventurous sort. He took a raft trip down the Grand Canyon. The trip sounded intriguing, so the following summer we went. The experience was wonderful. Most advertisements feature the excitement of the rapids and white water. The highlights of the trip for us were the quiet times, floating calmly on the river, admiring the gorgeous scenery, the subtle light changes through the day, and sleeping in sleeping bags under starlit skies. The helicopter ride out of the canyon matched all the excitement of the most tempestuous rapids.

Beman Pound, our art director, recommended small-boat cruising to the Inside Passage in Alaska. We enjoyed it so much, we did it a total of three times. However, once you have seen twelve glaciers, the excitement is gone. For us, whale sightings never lost their charm.

Bill Kortlander, a professor of art history and painting at Ohio University, suggested that we visit the J. M. W. Turner collection at the Tate Art Museum in London. Turner was born at the time of the American Revolution. Some of his late paintings are remarkable as examples of early impressionism. You might imagine that he was a friend of Monet, who lived a hundred years later.

Babs and Howard Sirak had the finest art collection in Columbus. Babs was the chair of Planned Parenthood when I served on the board. One evening after dinner, they showed us the Van Gogh painting they recently bought. That night they recommended that we visit the Kroller-Muller Museum in Holland. The museum contains almost as many Van Goghs as the Van Gogh Museum in Amsterdam. The collection is housed in a wonderful contemporary building in the Veluwe, a state park in the center of the country. We have been there twice.

When we lived in Palo Alto, Stanford had three nationally known painters as professors: Frank Lobdell, Nate Oliviera, and Keith Boyle. Keith was our neighbor, and we became friends. He often spoke about a delightful place on the Mendocino Coast called Sea Ranch, a resort destination designed by well-known architects from San Francisco. When we decided to move to California, we wondered whether Sea Ranch might be the place to live. Marian and I rented a house for six weeks in the middle of a rainy winter to test that option. Highway 1 was washed out above and below the ranch. After six weeks we concluded that it was too isolated for permanent residence, and we abandoned the idea. Nevertheless, we have vacationed there many times for long weekends with family, friends, or alone. Keith Boyle's suggestion was one of his greatest gifts to us.

If you listen carefully, friends can provide more than friendship. You can steal the best of their experiences and enrich your own.

Good hunting!

THE TORTURE OF A THOUSAND DROPS OF WATER

On October 9, 2009, Marian said she was going to the bathroom and walked out into the hallway. A few moments later, she came back in and said, "That's not the bathroom." So began a long, slow, and steady descent into moderate dementia. My mother had Alzheimer's disease that started with confusion.

For a long time, Marian and I did not talk about the issue. Then one day during a visit to our internist, the topic came up. Dr. Eisenberg recommended a neurological assessment, including an MRI of Marian's brain. During the interview with the psychologist, Marian missed only a few of the test questions: "Where are you?" "What day of the week is it?" "Who is president?" My daughter and I recognized Marian's confusion, but it was not debilitating. The MRI showed scars of some old ministrokes (TIAs), not Alzheimer's, and we resumed our normal lives. But 2009 was a bad health year for Marian: atrial fibulation, cellulitis infection in her right leg, and some other physical issues.

I could no longer give her the help she needed, such as putting on compression stockings every day, and we moved together to assisted living where Certified Nurse Assistants (CNAs) could help us with day-to-day needs. Marian started sleeping for long periods during the day, attributed at the time to thyroid imbalance. Marian walked with a walker around the apartment and used an electric scooter for long distances.

Then 2013 turned bleak. By September, Marian was having trouble walking, even with her walker. Her legs started buckling, and she fell frequently, but she was never hurt seriously.

Marian had persistent cellulitis in her right leg for years. The leg remained red and sometimes swollen. After one fall the nurse took her temperature. It was 103, and she was hustled off to the hospital. Her leg was seriously infected, and they began IV antibiotic. After four or five days, she was transferred to our healthcare center, where the IV antibiotic continued.

Weak but infection free, she came back to the apartment. She never regained strength. A nurse was required to attend her for every move: to her chair, to bed, to the bathroom. Marian did not accept her frailty and would get out of bed by herself. In December she fell three times. I was frightened. She was a dead weight, and I could not hold her up.

In early 2014, the management informed me that they could no longer assure me that Marian could be safe in assisted living. Marian was moved to the healthcare center. Her walking has not improved, even with aggressive physical therapy. Now, six months later, Marian is still in the healthcare center. She still cannot walk more than a step, even with a walker.

Our golden years are tarnished.

There's a Hole
in My Bucket

I woke thinking about what I wanted to do on my bucket list of things you should before you die: a trip to New Zealand perhaps, snorkeling in the Caymans, skydiving, etc. I concluded I preferred a "reverse bucket list," reliving highlights of things I have already done and would like to do again.

A Walk in the Woods in May

A walk in our farm woods in early May was exhilarating. Leaving the house, I relished the huge thirty-foot dogwood tree blooming near the pond. Our long lane traversed through woods before reaching the road. Along the wooded gravel lane, Dutchman's-breeches were profuse. If you looked to the left walking toward the road, the floor of the entire woods looked white with delicate spring beauties.

The land falls off sharply to the right. That's where the yellow dog-toothed violets bloomed on the steep slope near the creek. After enjoying the yellow violets, I hiked to the northern edge of the farm where the trillium were in full bloom, mostly white with a few rare red ones here and there. Nearby I searched for purple wild ginger in bloom hiding under last fall's leaves.

Happiness was a walk in the woods when these and many other wild flowers delighted me.

Gastronomy in Geneva

The downtown Movenpick restaurant in Geneva is not upscale. I ordered a hamburger, rare. Was there ever a better hamburger? It was served without a bun, juices flowing, smothered in a pile of caramelized onions, on top of which was a hefty serving of tangy sour cream.

On the other side of Lake Geneva, high on the hill, sat the World Health Organization, with a remarkable gourmet cafeteria that would shame most American restaurants. At the beverage counter, for example, a variety of chilled half-bottles of wine were offered to accompany the three-star cooking. The array of breads and cheeses were worth the elevator ride to the top-floor cafeteria overlooking the Lake Leman with the French Alps at the horizon.

Directly across the lake, and a brief taxi ride from Geneva, the restaurant Auberge du Lion d'Or prepared the evening's fare, an appetizer of delicate roget (a small, delicate red fish) sauced with an orange glaze; the entrée, roast lamb enhanced with fresh herbs picked from the garden on the hill below; and for dessert, a large martini glass of tiny wild strawberries doused with heavy cream. Forget the cost—you just had a peek of heaven.

Sanibel in January

Ranking high on my backward-facing bucket list is my desire to relive our long relationship with our timeshare condominium in Sanibel, Florida. We went there every year in January from the mid-1980s until 2006.

We never were water people. Fishermen were something to watch for entertainment, including the pelicans waiting for a handout—the innards of the gutted catch. We never longed for a sailboat or for snorkeling, although we would swim in the condo's swimming pool when the weather was hot.

Our building was fifty feet from the bay, with the open ocean a few hundred yards to the right. The views offered eye candy in all directions. Ospreys flew overhead, dolphins cruised by, children splashed in the pool as we sat in the Jacuzzi, bright red bougainvillea bloomed nearby.

We learned to unwind every January and to spend our days busy with trips to the grocery store, buying shrimp and key lime pies to accompany homemade comfort food dinners, often with close friends or relatives.

Once a week we visited the Ding Darling National Wildlife Refuge to search for rare water birds or the one visiting crocodile among the many alligators. The former mayor of Sanibel, "Bird" Westall, conducted canoe trips through the refuge that had to be scheduled at high tide because shallow water prevented passage through remote banyan growth if the tide was out.

California is too far from Florida, and we sold all four weeks for a nice profit. The delightful memories linger.

Cruising Vacations

Marian and I had never cruised while I was working. That changed when I retired in 1993. My boss recommended a cruise on the largest catamaran in the world, the Diamond Raddison, one hundred feet across the beam and four hundred feet long. Someone else recommended small-boat cruising; others recommended the Inside Passage as a destination.

After 1993, we took a small-boat cruise to Alaska and were smitten by the beauty. That was followed by a cruise at least once a year until we moved to California.

We traveled from Istanbul to Haifa, Stockholm to Finland, and Russia and to Portugal. We circumnavigated the United Kingdom, leaving from Edinburgh, sailing around the island and landing back in London; we cruised three times to Alaska. But the trips we enjoyed most were two transatlantic crossings that offered no ports of call and nothing but quiet relaxation and serene days. To fulfill my reverse bucket list, I would do those transatlantic crossings again with pleasure.

Bucket lists usually look forward. Mine look backward through a wonderful, satisfying life.

At eighty-five, I don't plan ahead with much enthusiasm. I do reminisce about the polar bears in Churchill, Manitoba, and the raft trip down the Grand Canyon.

However, I know my eventual destination.

LET'S STAY IN TOUCH

Eons ago two cavemen were sitting in a cave. One wanted to attract the other's attention. He picked up a rock and hit the other in the head. "Hey," said the aggrieved man, and language was born. Interactions among humanoids developed quickly as the grunts became differentiated and meant specific things.

Fast-forward to 2014.

Two teenagers are sitting in the school cafeteria. One says to the other, "You've got a cute little booty. I saw it on your Facebook page this morning." The other says, "I had 11,234 hits yesterday." This is modern communication at its most enlightened.

When I was young, the telephone was the most convenient means we had for remote contact. If you dialed 0, a nice lady would talk with you and then look up and dial a long distance number for you. We dialed another number and learned the correct time. We frequently played pranks. Call the drug store and ask whether they had Sir Walter Raleigh in a can. When the druggist said yes, you hollered, "Let him out" and hung up. What fun.

If you received a telegram, a man showed up at your door to deliver it. Yes, we really did receive singing telegrams on birthdays and holidays. Singing telegrams were big deals. The Western Union agent sang "Happy Birthday" standing at the front door. We could also send money via telegram during emergencies, and it would arrive the day it was sent. Very impressive.

After World War II, communication techniques changed rapidly. The Internet was created as a means of international data and message transfer. Home desktop computers were soon available, enabling something called "e-mail." We could write a letter, push the "send" button, and have it instantly delivered to friends or relatives anywhere in the world.

Wireless cell phones came to market that were bulky at first and eventually were reduced to the size of a wallet. Their complexity soared until they became very powerful computers and were labeled "smart phones." They were astounding. Their software contained hundreds of applications, nicknamed "apps." If you wanted to rent a condominium in Maui or a bed and breakfast in Oxford, England, it could be done in moments without leaving your kitchen.

An entirely new revolutionary communication concept emerged, entitled "social media." People could interact with relatives, friends, or strangers anywhere. People, particularly teenagers, discovered a new craze. "I can make a million friends and become famous overnight by revealing my innermost thoughts." Websites like Facebook, LinkedIn, Instagram, YouTube, and others encouraged humans to interact at a personal, intimate level.

Short forms of messaging became popular. Tweeting became rampant. Send a message in 140 characters. But before you do you, must learn an entirely new dictionary of abbreviations. For example, "YOYO" means "You're on your own." "HAND" means "Have a nice day." "TMB" means "Tweet me back."

Some pundits have raised the question of whether the teenage craze for social media is a pathologic form of narcissism enabled by the Internet. Probably it is, if it becomes obsessive. Teenagers are eager to create an adult identity, and tweeting helps—unless, of course, the teenager sends a lewd sexual fantasy that is bound to embarrass that person when he or she turns thirty.

I don't and won't tweet, join Facebook, or take part in any of the hundreds of opportunities to create a worldwide identity. I enjoy my little world whose scope is narrow. Sending e-mail and writing VIN YETS are my way of communicating, plus an occasional phone call.

Enough about communication for now.

HAND!

THINGS FALL APART

Things Fall Apart, the masterpiece novel by Chinua Achebe, describes the story of a tribal leader in Nigeria who is exiled to his wife's family home after an unfortunate accident. When he returns to his tribe after seven years, he finds that the British soldiers and Christian missionaries have changed the traditional Nigerian culture. He cannot adjust and commits suicide. The drastic changes could never be reversed. Everything had fallen apart for Okonkwo.

We are reminded that in old age everything literally falls apart. Golden years? I would like to strangle the SOB who said these are the golden years. Each day brings a new pain, often fleeting and inexplicable. Each day brings the loss of a last name of a friend with whom you spent weeks. Each month brings news of the death of someone you shared jokes with. Every six months you add a new prescription drug for an unexpected disease. Others are plagued with searing shingles or an infected sore that won't heal.

Can it be otherwise? Not really. Our circumstances are dictated by our life spans. It's a one-way street.

Things fall apart, even my couch. A few months ago, I was sitting in my usual spot when I heard a thump, and I was suddenly sitting four inches lower. The bottom had fallen out. That's life! I like the couch very much and want another just like it. A computer search at the Thomasville site revealed a similar one. "Your couch may still be on warranty. We will call you." So far, no call, and of course I threw away the purchase documents years ago. For the time being, I sit and wait, sunk in my hole. Why don't I move to the other side of the couch? Because I can't see the TV from there. Life is so crazy. (The couch was on warranty, and has been repaired.)

When Marian was moved to the healthcare center, I had an immediate sense that life had fallen apart. Actually, it did, and I began feeling sorry for myself. I had slept with the same woman for fifty-nine years, and she was gone. Then I looked around. Many of my friends have lost their spouses and have experienced similar feelings. Some friends have cancer, some are in pain. Many are lonely. Grow up, Tom. Welcome to the downside of old age.

The Chinese have perfected the idea of yin and yang, the interconnectedness of good and bad, happiness and sadness, good times and bad times. Marian and I have had mostly ups in our lives, and now we are experiencing bad times. Life is balancing out.

The Chinese also say that there is some bad in good times and some good in bad times. Now in bad times, I get to feed the cat. He loves me even more than he ever did.

Think about it!

Money, Money, Money

Let's be honest, we all like money. But our money is like a phantom: it is evaporating.

In the 1930s, Granddad went to the bank a few days before Christmas to obtain new one-dollar bills to give to his grandchildren. His annual gift made us feel rich. We could buy a lot of things with one dollar, such as penny candy. You could buy two spearmint leaves, two Mary Janes, or a licorice stick for a penny. A nickel would buy a Babe Ruth candy bar. A dollar went a long, long way.

Money was an important part of our education, and we were encouraged to save it. Small banks graced our bedrooms, some with keys and some with slots only. (When you needed money, you inserted a knife into the slot, shook vigorously, and hoped a nickel would slip out. I never considered this action immoral! It was my money.)

Elementary school teachers opened saving accounts for you at a real bank. Parents provided ten cents a week, submitted by the school. You checked your growing balance each week in your personal bankbook. Savings evoked thrift and represented the future, some expenditure to come. Unfortunately, the saved money always disappeared somehow, somewhere.

As a teenager I received my first employment check from the veterinary clinic where I cleaned cages. The check for fifteen dollars had my name typed on it, confirming my existence and my labor. For the first time, I had enough money to buy a game or go to a movie that I could pay for. Inflation was not a concern.

When we married in 1955, our first house cost $17,000. The hospital bill when our girls were born was $200 each—a bargain. My first job as an adult paid $175 a month. Inflation was 2 or 3 percent a year, but it compounded each year, raising prices. Today's prices leave me dumbfounded. I believe that a twenty-dollar bill should buy Nevada.

I worked a total of forty-three years for a division of Abbott Laboratories. We lived from paycheck to paycheck. Marian worked as a teacher, except when our girls were very little. That second income enabled us to have some luxuries in life, to own a timeshare condominium in Florida, to have two cars, etc. The company rewarded me with yearly stock options. That stock has become the core my estate.

In 1971 we bought a very large house in Palo Alto, for $65,000. We sold it three years later for $127,000. That house eventually came on the market for $3,400,000. I am amazed at what inflation has done to prices. A nickel candy bar now costs eighty cents or more. Gasoline costs four dollars a gallon. A cup of fancy coffee at Starbucks costs six dollars. A 2,000-square-foot-house in Saratoga, California, costs a million dollars or more. Inflation has left me in disbelief. My inner child of the past still believes that five dollars is a lot of money. The word *trillion* is beyond my comprehension.

The US Treasury is considering eliminating the penny because it no longer has sufficient value. Not in my mind. What's next, the dollar bill? What is inflation doing to us?

The stock market grows. As we get richer, we get poorer.

How odd.

Supplies for the Elderly

hearing aids

magnifying glasses

list of medications

stool softeners

incontinence supplies

canes, walkers, and electric scooters

clocks with large numbers

sleeping aids

et cetera

Afterword

The comedian Jerry Seinfeld claimed that his sitcom was about nothing. He meant that watchers didn't expect Plato or Kant each week but a little diversion and a little humor. Nothing too serious. My offerings are in the same vein. These books will never be best sellers or even end up on a remainders table. (Believe me.) As I write I think of all the people I have known—neighbors, fellow workers, choir members, mentors, relatives, friends, and others—who have been interesting but casual acquaintances. It would be wonderful if I could sit with all of you and have a thoughtful discussion.

Everyone has opinions about what is happening in our culture. Because of instant communication via the Internet, the culture sometimes seems to be changing too fast, even spinning out of control—or is that because I am eighty-five?

Life is strange and often amusing. The other day I read this headline: "Three-year-old accused of armed robbery." That's so bizarre that it leaves me speechless, but it might be the source of another VIN YET. You never know when events will trigger another writing session about nothing.

Like all humans, we have ups and downs, good times and bad times, happiness and sadness. But as the song reminds us, "Ole man river, he just keeps rolling along."

Tom McCollough

Summer 2014